LIFE SCIENCE FAIR PROJECTS

JORDAN MCGILL

www.av2books.com

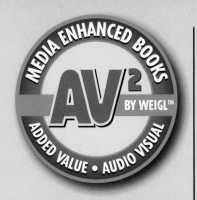

AV² provides enriched content that supplements and complements this book. Weigl's AV² books strive to create inspired learning and engage young minds in a total learning experience.

Your AV² Media Enhanced books come alive with...

Audio
Listen to sections of the book read aloud.

Key Words
Study vocabulary, and complete a matching word activity.

Video
Watch informative video clips.

Quizzes
Test your knowledge.

Embedded Weblinks
Gain additional information for research.

Slide Show
View images and captions, and prepare a presentation.

Try This!
Complete activities and hands-on experiments.

... and much, much more!

Go to **www.av2books.com**, and enter this book's unique code.

BOOK CODE

Q794382

AV² by Weigl brings you media enhanced books that support active learning.

Published by AV² by Weigl Publishers Inc.
350 5th Avenue, 59th Floor
New York, NY 10118
Website: www.av2books.com   www.weigl.com

Library of Congress Cataloging-in-Publication Data

McGill, Jordan.
 Life science fair projects / Jordan McGill.
    p. cm. -- (Science fair projects)
 Includes index.
 ISBN 978-1-61690-654-2 (hardcover : alk. paper) -- ISBN 978-1-61690-658-0 (softcover : alk. paper) -- ISBN 978-1-61690-330-5 (online)
 1. Life sciences--Experiments--Juvenile literature. 2. Science--Methodology--Juvenile literature. 3. Science projects--Juvenile literature. 4. Science fairs--Juvenile literature. I. Title.
 QH316.5.M34 2012
 570.72'4--dc22
                            2011014150

Printed in the United States of America in North Mankato, Minnesota
1 2 3 4 5 6 7 8 9 0   15 14 13 12 11

Project Coordinator Jordan McGill
Art Director Terry Paulhus

052011
WEP290411

CONTENTS

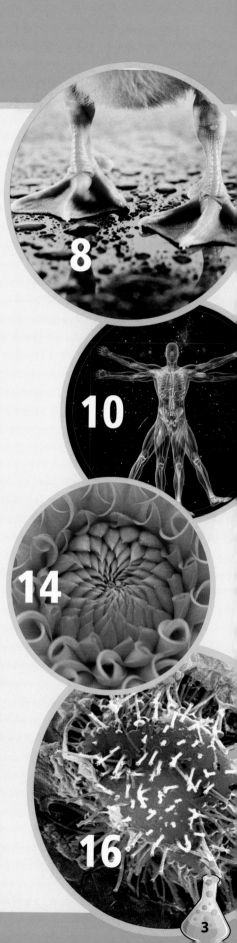

Take Part in a Science Fair

WHAT IS A SCIENCE FAIR?

A science fair is an event where students use the **scientific method** to create projects. These projects are then presented to spectators. Judges examine each project and award prizes for following the scientific method and preparing detailed displays. Some science fair winners move on to compete at larger fairs.

WHY SHOULD YOU TAKE PART IN A SCIENCE FAIR?

Science fairs are an excellent way to learn about topics that interest you. Winning is not the only reason to compete at a science fair. Science fairs are an opportunity for you to work hard on a project and show it off. You will also get to see the projects other students are presenting and learn from them as well.

ANYTHING ELSE I SHOULD KNOW?

Before you start, you should begin a logbook. A logbook is a handwritten diary of the tasks you performed to complete your science fair project. Include any problems or interesting events that occur.

WHERE DO I FIND A SCIENCE FAIR?

There are many fairs around the country and worldwide. Ask your teacher if he or she knows of any science fairs being held in your city. Once you find a fair to compete in, you can start preparing your project.

Eight Steps to a Great Science Fair Project

STEP 1
Select a topic

To begin, you must select a topic. Choose a topic that you would like to learn about. That way, working on the project will be exciting.

STEP 2
Form a question about your topic

Think of a question you have about your topic. You can ask, "What do plants need to grow?" You could also ask "Why can ducks swim so well?"

STEP 3
Research your question

Visit a library, and go online to research your topic. Keep track of where you found your **sources** and who wrote them. Most of your time should be spent learning about your topic.

STEP 4
Think about the answer to your question

Form a **hypothesis** that may answer your question. The sentence, "Plants need sunlight, water, and carbon dioxide to grow" is a hypothesis.

STEP 5
Plan an experiment to test your hypothesis

Design an **experiment** that you can repeat and that has observable **reactions**. Make a detailed plan of what you will do in your experiment and what materials you will need. Also include what you will be looking for when you do your experiment.

STEP 6
Conduct your experiment and record data

Carry out your experiment, and carefully observe what happens. Take notes. Record **data** if you need to. If you have nothing to note or record, reconsider whether your experiment has observable reactions.

STEP 7
Draw conclusions from your data

Were your predictions right? Sometimes, your hypothesis will be proven wrong. That is fine. The goal is to find the truth, not to be correct. When wrong, scientists think of a new hypothesis and try again.

STEP 8
Prepare a report and display

Write a report that explains your project. Include the topic, question, materials, plan, predictions, **data**, and conclusion in your report. Create a display that you can show at the science fair.

Picking a Life Science Topic

Life science is the study of all the living things on Earth. Many types of scientists, including **biologists**, **microbiologists**, and **botanists**, study life science.

This book offers sample experiments for each of the six earth science topics listed below. These experiments can be used to develop a science fair project. Select a topic that interests you. Then, use the sample experiment in this book for your project. You can also think of your own experiment that fits the topic.

TOPIC 1 BIRDS

Birds are feathered animals that lay eggs and have beaks. Scientists study birds to gain insight into bird biology.

TOPIC 2 HUMAN BODY

Like every animal, humans have a body that houses many complex **systems**. Whether studying the brain, the heart, or the lungs, there is much to examine. Researchers study the human body to better people's lives.

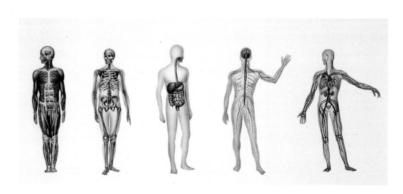

TOPIC 3 INSECTS

Insects are small **arthropods** with six legs. Many insects also have wings. Although scientists have found only one million kinds of insect **species**, there could be as many as 10 million. People study insects to learn more about their behavior and find more species.

TOPIC 4 PLANTS

Bushes, grasses, herbs, mosses, trees, and vines are all plants. Plants are studied in hopes of finding new medicines and to better understand how Earth's environment functions.

TOPIC 5 BACTERIA

Bacteria are incredibly small **organisms** that are found everywhere on Earth. There are up to one billion bacteria **cells** in one ounce (gram) of soil. Scientists study bacteria to cure disease and make new technology.

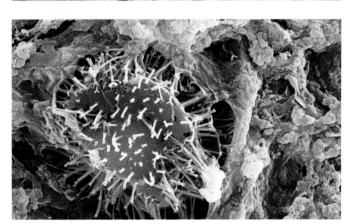

TOPIC 6 FOOD CHAIN

All creatures are members of a food chain, even humans. Food chains map an animal's place in its environment. Studying animals helps people understand how all of Earth's creatures are dependent on each other.

Why Can Ducks Swim so Well?

Background Information

The world is home to many species of birds. While they may look very different, all birds share several common features. For instance, all birds lay eggs and have beaks. They also have feathers covering their body.

Birds live all over the world. Some live in tropical forests and in hot deserts. Others live at sea. Some even live in the cold polar regions of Earth. Birds can live in such varied **habitats** because they have **adapted** to them. They have developed special features to help them live in their environment.

EXPERIMENT

In this experiment, you will examine one type of bird adaptation. Ducks can fly, but they also spend a great deal of time in water. They use their webbed feet to push through the water. This allows them to swim to the bottoms of ponds and lakes to catch food. The webs between a duck's toes increase water **resistance**. Without this adaptation, ducks would not live as they do.

TIP #1
Also experiment with the surface area of duck feet. The U-shaped cutout is smaller than the uncut lid. How well does it work?

TIP #2
Instead of yogurt lids, you can use another wide rubber object, such as a spatula. Just make sure that the rubber bends easily.

Test Duck Feet in 7 Steps

CAUTION

Sharp   Wet

DIFFICULTY

EASY   MEDIUM   HARD

TIME 40 minutes

MATERIALS
- 3 yogurt container lids
- Bathtub
- String
- Small object that floats
- Small object that sinks
- Scissors

INSTRUCTIONS

STEP 1 Cut a large U-shape into one of the lids. Be sure to leave room at the bottom so that you can hold it. There should only be 1 inch (2.3 centimeters) at most left on each side.

STEP 2 Cut one of the other lids into thin strips. Leave an uncut section at the bottom of the lid to hold on to. Leave the third lid whole.

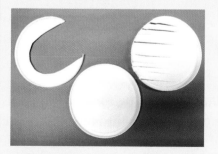

STEP 3 Tie one end of the string to the heavy object and the other end to the object that floats. The string should not reach the bottom of the bathtub.

STEP 4 Fill the bathtub with water.

STEP 5 Put the objects tied together with string into the tub. The heavier object should weigh enough to sink to the bottom.

STEP 6 Take one of the lids, and place your forearm into the water. Wave the lid back and forth. Use only your hand to wave. If you move your whole arm, your experiment's data will be off. Repeat this process with the other lids. Take notes on how much each lid moves the floating object.

STEP 7 The uncut lid is like a duck's webbed feet. The U-shaped lid is like a non-swimming bird's feet. Which lid worked best? Why?

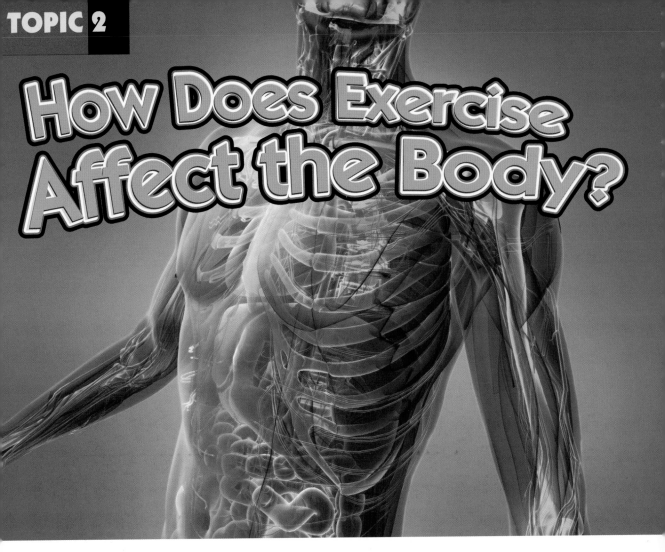

How Does Exercise Affect the Body?

Background Information

The human body works much like a machine. Every part depends on another part in order to do its job.

Structures inside and outside the human body protect it, help it move, and give it shape. **Muscles** and **bones** work together inside our bodies. They give our bodies support and strength. Skin, hair, and nails work as a protective outer layer.

The human body needs **nutrients** and oxygen to grow, do work, and repair itself. The lungs send oxygen from the air into blood. The heart then pumps blood to all the parts of the body. Blood carries nutrients and oxygen throughout the body. It moves through the body in a process called circulation.

EXPERIMENT

The human body has a complex system of muscles that contract and release to make it move. Muscles require energy and oxygen to contract. The faster the body moves, the harder the lungs and heart must work to power it.

In this experiment, you will perform tests on your own body to better understand how it works. This experiment requires some physical activity. Find a safe place outside to perform it.

TIP #1
If you have any difficulty breathing or being active, do not attempt this experiment.

TIP #2
If you have trouble finding your heart rate under the chin, try getting a pulse from your wrist.

Find Your Heart Rate in 4 Steps

CAUTION

Physical

DIFFICULTY

EASY — MEDIUM — HARD

TIME 30 minutes

MATERIALS
- Stopwatch
- Paper
- Pencil

INSTRUCTIONS

STEP 1 Practice finding your heart rate. Place two fingers on your neck under your chin. With the help of the stopwatch, count how many beats you feel in one minute. That is your heart rate. Do this three times to find an average. Record this number. It is your standing heart rate.

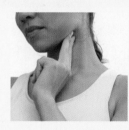

STEP 2 Exercise by running around, doing jumping jacks, or by lying down and standing up quickly. Do this until you are out of breath. Count how many beats you feel in one minute. Record this number. This is your heart rate after difficult activity.

STEP 3 Wait 10 minutes. Then, walk around for five minutes. Take it easy, you want to avoid losing your breath. Count how many beats you feel in one minute. Record this number. This is your heart rate after easy activity.

STEP 4 Compare the three heart rates. The heart beats faster when the body is performing difficult activities. As a result, it pumps more blood through the body to parts that need it. As more blood is pumped through the body, the lungs work harder to replace the body's oxygen supply. How does this extra work affect the body?

What Foods Do Ants Prefer?

Background Information

Insects are one of the largest groups of animals. There are more than one million types of insect species. They represent about half of all known living things. For every person in the world, there are about two billion insects.

Insects are often thought of as a bother, but they are actually very helpful animals. They help keep neighborhoods clean. When an animal dies or garbage is left outside, insects often eat the remains. If left to rot, these remains could make people or animals sick.

Ants are just one type of insect that helps clean up the environment. Have you ever left pieces of food on the ground during a picnic only to have them disappear? Ants clean up and eat food they find lying around. They are able to lift 20 times their body weight. When working as a team, ants can move large pieces of food. They often work together to survive.

EXPERIMENT

In this experiment, you will test how ants react to different types of food. The experiment requires that you prepare an enclosed area to observe the ants behavior. The closed area makes it easier to examine exactly what they prefer to eat.

Watch Ants in 5 Steps

CAUTION

Cost   Adult's Help

DIFFICULTY

EASY   MEDIUM   HARD

TIME 60 minutes

MATERIALS
- 10-20 Ants
- Large surface of cardboard or wax paper
- Apple
- Butter knife
- Sugar cube
- Salt
- Oatmeal
- Small piece of meat
- Leafs

INSTRUCTIONS

STEP 1 Lay cardboard or wax paper down to create a large surface for your experiment. This will allow you to see and track the ants more easily.

STEP 2 Place two pieces of food on the large surface. The foods should be different, but both pieces should be the same size. Place the ants onto the surface near the food. Which type of food attracts the ants?

STEP 3 Keep the food the ants liked from Step 2. Add a different piece of food. Do the ants want it more than their preferred food from Step 2? If so, match that piece of food with another, and test the ants again.

STEP 4 Run independent tests with each food by placing only one piece of food on the surface. There should be some foods that the ants have no interest in taking.

STEP 5 Continue to match foods against each other until you find which  food the ants prefer. Take notes on each match-up. Pay attention to which foods the ants avoid completely. Ants are drawn toward food that they can eat and use. Some foods will serve no purpose for them. What types of food did your ants eat? Did these foods have anything in common?

How Do Plants Grow?

Background Information

Plants help make Earth a living planet. Without plants, there would be no initial food source for animals to eat. Plants also make oxygen that animals breathe. More than 270,000 different kinds of plants live on Earth.

Most plants have three main parts, which are roots, stems, and leaves. Roots keep a plant anchored in the ground. They collect water and minerals from the soil.

Stems hold a plant's leaves up to gather sunlight. They also move water, food, and minerals to different places inside the plant.

EXPERIMENT

TIP #1

Any fast-growing seed can be used in the experiment.

P lants need three things to make food—sunlight, water, and carbon dioxide. Inside their leaves, plants have a green-colored substance called chlorophyll. Chlorophyll helps leaves make food for the plant.

Chlorophyll lets plants use sunlight to change water and carbon dioxide into sugar. Sugar is the food plants make to feed themselves. Plants use food to grow and stay healthy. In this experiment, you will learn how a plant's growth is affected when it lacks one of its three necessities.

TIP #2

A graph is a useful way to show how much each seed has grown. On the vertical axis, record the plant's height. On the horizontal axis, record what day the measurement was taken. Use a different color for each plant.

Grow Plants in 9 Steps

CAUTION

Messy   Wet

DIFFICULTY

EASY   MEDIUM   HARD

TIME 60 minutes + 3 weeks of observation

MATERIALS
- Four 500 ml milk cartons
- Bean or corn seeds
- Soil
- Scissors
- Water
- Ruler

INSTRUCTIONS

STEP 1 Cut the tops off the milk cartons.

STEP 2 Fill all four cartons 3/4 full with soil.

STEP 3 Plant one seed in each carton. Dampen the soil with 2 tablespoons of water.

STEP 4 Wait for the **seedlings** to sprout.

STEP 5 Place one container in a dark space with no light, such as a cupboard. You must water this plant.

STEP 6 Place one container in sunlight, but seal it in a clear plastic bag. You will water this plant as well.

STEP 7 Place the third container in sunlight. You will not water this plant.

STEP 8 Place the final container in sunlight. You will water this plant. This plant is the control group. It has access to all it should need to grow.

STEP 9 As the seedlings begin to sprout from the soil, measure them every three days to keep track of how much they have grown. Use the ruler to get an accurate measurement. Note your findings. After several weeks, compare the plants' growth. Which plant has grown the most? Which plant showed the least growth? Why do you think this happened?

Where Does Bacteria Grow?

Background Information

Bacteria can be found almost anywhere, such as on counters, in snow, and even on skin and in the human body. Most often, bacteria can only be seen with a **microscope**. Bacteria are the world's simplest creatures. Their sole purpose is to create more bacteria.

Although bacteria simply try to make more of themselves, they end up doing much more. Some are helpful. They help animals digest food and allow plants to absorb nutrients. Others are dangerous. Bacteria cause many diseases found in plants and animals. These single-celled creatures cause more disease and death in humans than any other **parasite**.

EXPERIMENT

Many of the bacteria in your body are necessary and helpful. Some other bacteria can make you sick. Every time you touch a door knob, railing, or keyboard, bacteria gets on your hands. In this experiment, you will take samples from around the house to see which areas grow the most bacteria.

Grow Bacteria in 7 Steps

CAUTION

Cost

DIFFICULTY

EASY   MEDIUM   HARD

TIME 40 minutes + 1 week of observation

MATERIALS
- Chicken or beef broth
- Sugar
- 4 Petri dishes
- Plastic container
- 4 cotton swabs
- Masking tape
- Pen or marker

INSTRUCTIONS

STEP 1 Add a very thin layer of broth, no more than 0.5 inches (1 millimeter), to the bottom of each Petri dish.

STEP 2 Wet the tops of your cotton swabs. Go around the house, and rub each swab against one object. Some places to try are the kitchen counter, a drain in a sink, a doorknob, or a computer keyboard.

STEP 3 Rub each swab in a Petri dish. Ensure that the swabs do not touch each other and that each Petri dish only comes in contact with one swab. Seal each Petri dish.

STEP 4 Use the masking tape to make labels for each Petri dish. Write where each sample came from on the tape.

STEP 5 Place the Petri dishes in the plastic container. Seal the plastic container.

STEP 6 Place the plastic container in a warm, dark area.

STEP 7 Check on your bacteria every day, and keep notes. After a week or two, record which location produced the most bacteria. Why do you think bacteria grows in such quantity here? Experiments like this show the importance of hand washing. Imagine how much bacteria can be found in public places.

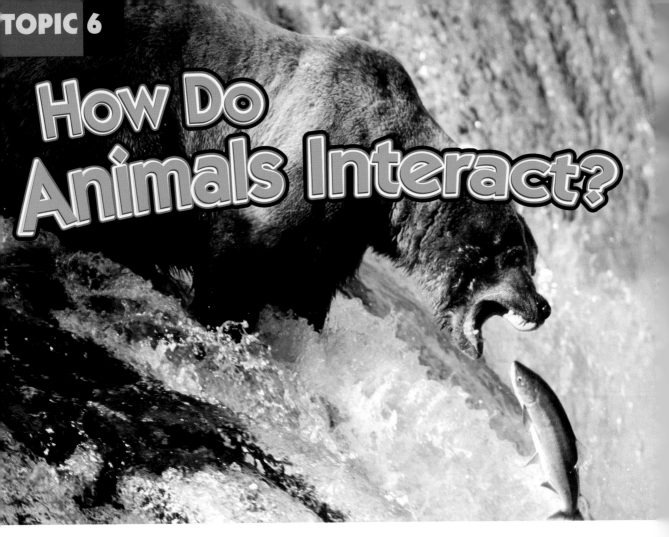

How Do Animals Interact?

Background Information

All living things depend on each other to survive. Food chains show how animals survive by eating other plants or animals. Energy is transferred from one living thing to another further along the food chain.

One example of a food chain starts with a plant. Tiny insects called aphids live on plants and eat the juices from their stems. The aphids are eaten by bigger insects, such as ladybugs. The ladybugs, in turn, may be food for birds. Then, larger animals, such as wolves, eat the birds.

A food web is a combination of many food chains. Most animals have more than one food source. As multiple food chains begin to connect, a food web is created.

EXPERIMENT

Food webs are made up of producers and consumers. Plants are the only producers. This is because they make energy. This energy is used by the consumers. Consumers feed on plants and each other to survive. Food webs are made up of many consumers and producers interacting.

In this experiment, you will create a food web and see how animals interact in a complex community. Without these interactions, animals would not be able to survive.

Link a Food Web in 5 Steps

TIP #1
This experiment can be done like a game. Have two people try to connect two animals in as few steps as possible.

TIP #2
Try a library or look online for useful research tools.

DIFFICULTY

EASY — MEDIUM — HARD

TIME 60 minutes

MATERIALS
- Large piece of construction paper
- Markers
- Glue
- Research materials
- Scissors
- Nature magazine
- Vinegar

INSTRUCTIONS

STEP 1 Search through the magazine, and cut out two different animals that live in the same part of a country. If you pick an animal that only lives in **tundra** and another that lives in desert, you might not be able to connect them. Try to pick one herbivore, an animal that eats plants, and one carnivore, an animal that eats other animals.

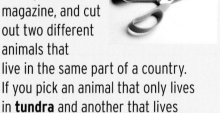

STEP 2 Research the two animals. Note where they live. Glue each animal to opposite ends of the construction paper.

STEP 3 For each animal, write down two things that it eats and two things that eat it on the construction paper.

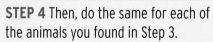

STEP 4 Then, do the same for each of the animals you found in Step 3.

STEP 5 Continue to find out what each animal eats until you connect the two animals you initially picked. How many animals did you need before you made the connection?

Preparing Your Report

Once your experiment is completed, write a report. The purpose of the report is to summarize your work. You want others to understand the question, the research, and the experiment. The report also explains your results and ties everything together in a conclusion.

1 Title
The title of your report should be the question you are trying to answer.

2 Purpose
This section of the report should include a few sentences explaining why you chose this project.

3 Hypothesis
The hypothesis is made up of one sentence that explains the answer your experiment was meant to prove.

4 Background
Write a summary of the information you found during your research. You most likely will not need to use all of your research.

5 Materials
Write a list of the materials you used during your experiment. This is the same as the list of materials included with each sample experiment in this book.

6 Plan
Write out the steps needed to carry out your experiment.

7 Results
Write all observations and relevant data you recorded during your experiment here. Include any tables or graphs you made.

8 Conclusion
In this part of the report, state what you learned. Be sure to write how you think your results prove or disprove your hypothesis. You should also write your hypothesis again somewhere in this section. It is acceptable if your hypothesis was false. What is important is that you were creative and followed the scientific method.

9 Bibliography
Include an alphabetical list by the author's last name of all sources you used.

Making Your Display

Most science fairs encourage the use of a backboard to display your project. Most displays use a three-panel backboard. It stands up on its own and is easy to view.

- On your backboard, include most of the material from your report. Leave out the background information. You may also include photos or drawings to help explain your project.

- Most often, your backboard will be placed on a table. On the table, you can include any models you created or samples you collected. Also include the logbook and a copy of your report.

- If possible, you may also perform your experiment at the fair.

Impressing the Judges

Know the Rules

Judges expect that you know the rules. Breaking rules can lead to lost points and even **disqualification**. Rules will change depending on who is organizing the science fair. Before you begin your project, talk to the organizers of the fair you plan to compete in. Ask them for a list of rules.

* Most fairs do not allow any dangerous materials, such as flames or organisms that could make someone sick.

Practice Presenting

To stand out at the science fair, you have to give a strong presentation to the judges. Write a short speech that covers what you want to say. Your speech should summarize why you chose the project. It should also explain the experiment and your **conclusions**. Practice this speech until you are comfortable. Speak confidently and clearly.

* Many judges will ask questions. Present your project to friends and family. Then, have them ask questions as if they were judges.

Dress For an Event

A science fair is a special event. It is different from an ordinary day. When you go somewhere special, do your parents have you dress up? Judges look at every part of your presentation, including you. Wear something special. Comb your hair. Tuck in your shirt. Tie your shoes. You are presenting yourself as much as your project.

Glossary

adapted: adjusted to make suitable

arthropods: a type of invertebrate, which is an animal without a backbone

biologists: researchers who study living organisms

bones: the hard pieces that form a skeleton

botanists: researchers who study plants

cells: units that make up all organisms

conclusions: the results or outcomes of an act or process

data: items of information

disqualification: to be eliminated from a competition

experiment: a test, trial, or procedure

habitats: living environments for certain organisms

hypothesis: a possible explanation for a scientific question

microbiologists: researchers who study microorganisms

microscope: a tool used to see very small microorganisms

muscles: tissue in animals that allows that contracts and allows the animal to move

nutrients: substances found in food that allow people to maintain their health

organism: any living things

parasite: an organism that grows, feeds, and is sheltered on or in a different organism while contributing nothing to the survival of its host

reactions: when two or more substances combine to make a new chemical substance

resistance: a force that opposes motion

scientific method: a system of observation

seedlings: young plants

sources: the books or websites from which research was obtained

species: a class of organisms that share characteristics

systems: a set of things that work together

tundra: an environment where the ground is permanently frozen and there are no trees

Index

Log on to www.av2books.com

AV² by Weigl brings you media enhanced books that support active learning. Go to www.av2books.com, and enter the special code found on page 2 of this book. You will gain access to enriched and enhanced content that supplements and complements this book. Content includes video, audio, web links, quizzes, a slide show, and activities.

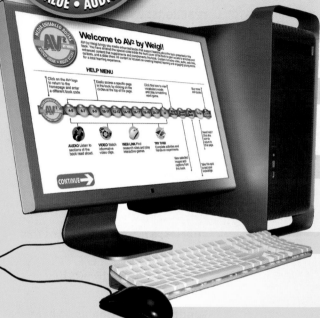

Audio
Listen to sections of the book read aloud.

Video
Watch informative video clips.

Embedded Weblinks
Gain additional information for research.

Try This!
Complete activities and hands-on experiments.

WHAT'S ONLINE?

Try This!	Embedded Weblinks	Video	EXTRA FEATURES
Create useful observation sheets.	Check out more information about life science topics.	Watch a video about life science.	**Audio** Listen to sections of the book read aloud.
Make a judging sheet.		Check out another video about life science.	
Make a timeline to make sure projects are finished on time.	Learn how to coordinate a science fair.		**Key Words** Study vocabulary, and complete a matching word activity.
Complete fun interactive life science activities.	Learn more about creating an effective display.		**Slide Show** View images and captions, and prepare a presentation.
			Quizzes Test your knowledge.

AV² was built to bridge the gap between print and digital. We encourage you to tell us what you like and what you want to see in the future.

Sign up to be an AV² Ambassador at www.av2books.com/ambassador.